REFLECTION OF HISTORY IN
BLOOD DIAMOND

The Power of Cinema

Reflection of History in Blood Diamond: The Power of Cinema

DB Thakuri

Published by DB Thakuri, 2023.

While every precaution has been taken in the preparation of this book, the publisher assumes no responsibility for errors or omissions, or for damages resulting from the use of the information contained herein.

REFLECTION OF HISTORY IN BLOOD DIAMOND: THE POWER OF CINEMA

First edition. October 12, 2023.

ISBN: 979-8223798538

Written by DB Thakuri.

Also by DB Thakuri

Reflection of History in Blood Diamond: The Power of Cinema

Reflection of History in Blood Diamond: The Power of Cinema

Headwaters of Screenwriting: The Art of Crafting Original Screenplays

Table of Contents

Reflection of History in Blood Diamond: The Power of Cinema 1

PREFACE 5

Preface | Chapter I: History and Its Reflection | Chapter II: Historical Reflection through New Historicism | Chapter III: Reflection of History in Blood Diamond | Chapter IV: Conclusion: A Call for Critical Assessment of History 7

Chapter I 8

Chapter II 22

Chapter III 38

Chapter IV 65

To my son, Shubham

DB THAKURI

COPYRIGHT

Copyright © 2023 by DB Thakuri

All rights reserved.

No part of this book may be reproduced in any form or by any means without the prior written permission of DB Thakuri.

Thakuri, DB, 1984 –

Reflection of History in Blood Diamond: The Power of Cinema / DB Thakuri.

REFLECTION OF HISTORY IN BLOOD DIAMOND: THE POWER OF CINEMA

To,
My son, Shubham Thakuri

3

ACKNOWLEDGMENTS

I would like to express my profound sense of gratitude to my book editor Mr. Chiranjibi Kafle, Lecturer and former Head of, the Department of English at Ratna Rajyalaxmi Campus, for his scholarly guidance and constructive suggestions to bring this book to its present form.

I am immensely grateful to my wife, Sabina Thakuri, and son, Shubham Thakuri for their eternal inspiration. Last but not certainly least; I am forever indebted to my parents for their incessant love and support.

PREFACE

Traditionally, history is regarded as the collection of factual events but literature is supposed to be the outcome of a literary writer's mere imagination. After the arrival of new historicism, it tries to blur the gap between history and fiction. This book looks into the cinema *Blood Diamond* (2006) from the perspective of new historicism. This film is based on Sierra Leone's history during the last decade of the 20th century and it captures the social and political reality as if a history in fictional form as the historical meta-fiction. In particular, it captures Sierra Leone's civil war from 1996 to 2001 and includes real historical incidents like trade and conflict associated with the diamond, the rise of the Revolutionary United Front (RIJF), the use of child soldiers in military activities, and a large number of killing and displacement. There is the actual reflection of the social and political realities of Sierra Leone and the unhealthy power practice and struggle for diamonds according to the greed of various political and non-political groups including western smugglers and tradesmen. All these scenes of the cinema are not beyond Sierra Leone's history. Keeping these historical facts reflected in *Blood Diamond* (2006) into consideration, this book, a parallel reading between facts and fiction based on a new historical perspective, concludes that cinema stands as a part of history blurring the gap between a work of art and historical facts.

Contents

Acknowledgments

Preface

Chapter I: History and Its Reflection

Chapter II: Historical Reflection through New Historicism

Chapter III: Reflection of History in Blood Diamond

Chapter IV: Conclusion: A Call for Critical Assessment of History

Works Cited

About the Author

Chapter I

History and Its Reflection

History

History, by meaning and definition, captures an inquiry, knowledge acquired by investigation. It is related to past events as well as memory, discovery, collection, organization, presentation, and interpretation of information about these events. Through the traditional definition, history refers to the collection of facts and events that occurred in the past. Historians write in the context of their own time, and with due regard to the current dominant ideas of how to interpret the past, and sometimes write to provide lessons for their society. Moreover, history is facilitated by the formation of a true discourse of the past through the production of narrative and analysis of past events relating to the human race. The modern discipline of history is dedicated to the institutional production of this discourse.

History can also refer to the academic discipline which uses a narrative to examine and analyze a sequence of past events, and objectively determine the patterns of cause and effect that determine them. According to Peter N. Stearns, Peters Seixas, and Sam Wincburg, "Historians sometimes debate the nature of history and its usefulness by discussing the study of the discipline as an end in itself and as a way of providing perspective on the problems of the present (6)

Thus, traditionally, history is regarded as the collection of facts events, and incidents. It presupposes that history is opposite to literature or fiction since literary work is supposed to be the

REFLECTION OF HISTORY IN BLOOD DIAMOND: THE POWER OF CINEMA

outcome of the author's imagination. After the arrival of new historicism, even the fact within history is questioned. For new historicists, history too is guided by power influence and discourse so it bears the quality of fiction. Fictional writing, on the other hand, is based on the social, cultural, and historical reality of the author's timeframe. In this sense, there is also historical reality within the literary writing. Thus, New Historicists try to blur the gap between history and fiction.

History in Literature

Now after the arrival of new historicism, there is a trend to mark history which is reflected in literature. The literature, now, has a relation with history because there is an influence of social, political, cultural, and historical reality upon the author. No writer can go completely beyond reality. The work of art cannot be a product of the mere imagination of the artist. Modem reading of literature has a reciprocal concern with the historicity of texts and the textuality of history. New historicists consider historical accounts as equally interpretable as literary texts since both are seen as expressions of the same historical moment. Literature itself stands as the history of the contemporary circumstances of its writing.

This book is based on the movie *Blood Diamond* (2006) and in particular, it tries to trace the reflection of Sierra Leone's part of history during the last decade of the 20th century as reflected in the film. As the political war thriller, co-produced and directed by Edward Zwick and written by Edward Zwick and Marshall Herskovitz starring Leonardo DiCaprio, Jennifer Connelly, and Djimon Hounsou, it captures Sierra Leone's civil war from 1996 to 2001 by portraying the politics behind the nch minerals like a diamond. The title *'Blood Diamond'* refers to the violent circumstances of Sierra Leone due to the unhealthy power practice and struggle for diamonds due to the interest and greed of various political and non-political groups, western smugglers, and tradesmen.

The film not only represents the true history of Sierra Leone but also depicts how the African countries are torn apart by violence and struggles and most of the natives have been living the lives of refugees and exiled due to the greed of various political and non-political groups, Western smugglers and tradesmen upon the treasures and valuable minerals like diamonds.

Sierra Leone in History

During the period between 1993 and 2001, Sierra Leone faced the critical situation of war and terror due to the civil war. A country was torn apart by the struggle between government loyalists and insurgents. Many of the atrocities of the war including the rebels' amputation of people's hands to discourage them from voting in upcoming elections, the violence associated with rich minerals as well as political instabilities, etc., are some of the key features of Sierra Leone that time. All these incidents stand as the true history of the country.

The illegal diamond supply to the West is the major aspect associated with the violence in Sierra Leone Jeremy Ginifer and Kaye Oliver write. "The historical conference concerning illegal diamonds refers to an actual meeting that took place in Kimberley, South Africa in 2000 too has focused on Sierra Leone's history associated with diamond and conflict" (27) According to Ginifer and Oliver, it led to the Kimberley Process Certification Scheme, which seeks to certify the origin of rough diamonds to curb the trade in conflict diamonds. In this sense, the fact behind the conflict in Sierra Leone is its rich minerals and diamonds. The social and political events that happened in Africa during the last decade of the 20th century are related to people's greed for diamonds. The diamond is associated with the history of Sierra Leone. The government of the United Kingdom also had its fair share to say about the prospects for peace in Sierra Leone with the connection of diamonds in Sierra Leone. Jeremy Ginifer and Kaye Oliver write:

> Diamonds and Other Economic Causes of Conflict: the use of diamonds to finance the conflict was a major conflict multiplier in Sierra Leone. Further, there is the potential for diamonds to be exploited again should another rebel group emerge. Moreover, the lack of government revenue being generated through diamond mining is hindering a recovery in Sierra Leone, although the 2003 figure will double that of 2002 (28).

The United Kingdom assumed that the illegal diamond supply was the major cause behind the violence in Sierra Leone. Thus, it stated, "The UK should continue to press for rapid progress in terms of GoSL taking control of the diamond sector. This is an area that will need to be closely monitored" (28) to halt the chaotic situation in Sierra Leone.

The history of Sierra Leone marks that the diamond is the primary reason behind the chaotic situation in Sierra Leone. It is a historical fact of the country. Westerners' extreme quest for diamonds and their involvement in illegal trade created various terrorist groups according to the design of international smugglers. On the other hand, the struggle between government loyalists and insurgent forces led the country to further destruction

The political conflicts of the nation, the fight between the government and terrorist groups, and the snuggling of diamonds are some of the real incidents connected with the contemporary time frame of Sierra Leone which ended in 2002. In this connection, Ibrahim Abdullah writes, "Taylor supported the March 1991 insurgency of the Revolutionary United Front (RUF) led by Foday Sankoh in neighboring Sierra Leone. That support continued until the official declaration of the end of hostilities in January 2002 (54).

In rebel group like RUF, there were the involvement of youths and teenagers Jeremy Ginifer and Kaye Oliver write, "Concerns remain that ex-combatants and youths currently engaged in diamond mining in the cast-potentially one of the future conflict hotspots in Sierra Leone may become a source of trouble if they disengage from diamond mining" (28). The primary reason behind the violence is natural resources like diamonds and others. In this connection, Daudi Mwakawago writes. "Sierra Leone faces a spectrum of challenges, from explosive youth unemployment to taking legitimate control of its rich mineral resources, as the United Nations peacekeeping mission winds down and the next phase of the West African country's development begins" (1).

Sierra Leone's history captures the nation which is torn apart by violence and terrorism. The terror of war in Sierra Leone is reflected within the image of rebels' amputation of people's hands to discourage them from voting in elections, the terrorist attack in the capital city, and the forceful recruitment of child soldiers and their use in attacks on innocent villagers. Similarly, millions of people are exiled from their land and kept as refugees in various camps throughout Sierra Leone's history.

Blood Diamond as the Historical Discourse

Discourse refers to all the utterances whether spoken or written that signify something at an underlying level including the generation of meaning through images, sounds, cultural performances, singing, dancing, games, etc. So discourse indicates images, sounds, and practices that are close to the sign system of language. Regarding the same issue, Stephen Slemon has quoted Edward Said, "What brought that purely conceptual space into being, argue Said, is a European style of thought based on an ontological and epistemological distinction made between the Orient and the Occident" (111-112), Michael Foucault regards that a writer creates a book and the process of writing deals with an attempt of generating discourse, the source of power.

Discourse is a system of the flexibility of acts by which influential groups in society construct the field of truth through the means of certain knowledge, values, and discipline upon marginalized ones. Excluding others' ideas and perspectives, discourse highlights the targeted aim by producing the objects of knowledge intellectually. Edward Said, in his book *Orientalism*, claims, "The relation between Occident and Orient is a relationship of power, of domination, of varying of a complex hegemony..." (5). He says that cultural discourse and exchange within a culture that is commonly circulated are not truth but only representations.

At the beginning of the 1970s, Michel Foucault started to develop his theory of power relations. His interest is framed not only within his own philosophical and intellectual project but, at the same time, reacted to the concerns of a society that was changing quickly. Foucault advances the principle of discourse in relation to the power structure acting in society by stating that discourses are deeply rooted in social organization that runs through discourse. So discourse and power cannot be isolated due to inseparable ties. Abrahams in his book *A Glossary of Literary Terms presents*, "Discourse has become the focal term among critics who oppose the destructive concept of a general text that functions independently of particular historical condition...Class structures and power relationships alter in the course of history" (262).

Foucault claims that the figure who until then had been considered to be a theorist could not be seen anymore as a subject and as a result of this, the intellectual was not to be seen anymore as the 'representative consciousness' of society. The theorist has ceased to be a subject, a representing and representative consciousness but not the actual representation of the objects. There is no longer any representation; there is only action, theory's action, and the action of practice in the relationships of networks

In this context, and in relation to his criticism of traditional Western epistemology, Foucault began to establish a stronger connection between the roles that intellectuals and culture play within the framework of power relations that construct the subject.He can be considered as one of the answers to the collapse of the classical theorization of, for instance, the Sartrean universal intellectual in the post-war period. Foucault rejects this idea because he considers that it is directly related to the idea of the existence of an absolute Truth with its corresponding essentialist and universal subject.

New historicism, on the one hand, captures the reflection of history within the text, and on the other, it tries to seek the discourses created by text through the perspective of hidden voices. *Blood Diamond*, the film captures both the dimensions of new historicism. On the one hand, it reflects the parts of the historical reality of Sierra Leone during the last decade of the 20th century. On the other hand, the film revives the hidden politics behind diamonds and minerals evoking the Westerners' interest in it, and tries to deal with the issues of how the common people like Solomon have been victimized due to the power politics and play between different terrorist groups and government forces.

Through the setting of Sierra Leone, the film depicts how African countries are torn apart by violence and struggles, and most of the natives have been living the lives of refugees and exiled due to their greed for treasures and valuable minerals like diamonds. In this sense, the power play for natural resources, the greed of foreigners, the suffering of marginal people, etc., are not beyond the realities of the African continent. The diamonds mined in Africa are the major cause of turning the country into a war zone so the diamond itself is the major discourse to bring the reality into the light through the film.

Blood Diamond brings the story of Sierra Leone from 1991 to 2001 capturing the social and political realities of the contemporary timeframe. It includes the issues of the search for diamonds and its consequences like civil wars, chaotic circumstances, violence, and murder of ordinary people and their refugee lives and exile, etc. All these incidents of Sierra Leone's history reflected in the scenes of the cinema represent a part of the history of Sierra Leone.

Reviews on Film

The film *Blood Diamond* has received keen attraction from various cine critics and academicians. One of the cine critics, Claudia Puig said in *USA Today*, "*Blood Diamond* is a gem in a season with lots of worthy movies" (8) He further praises DiCaprio's acting and noted that "It is also the first time the boyish actor has truly seemed like a man on the film"(8). Since DiCaprio has been playing a leading role in love stories and *Blood Diamond* is about the action and violence-oriented film Claudia Puig marks DiCaprio's shift in the film.

Like Puig, Peter Rainer also gives the film a positive review in the Christian Science Monitor. He also praised DiCaprio's acting, "As strong as *Blood Diamond* is in its best moments, I wish it had been even harder-edged. DiCaprio is remarkable-his work is almost on par with his performance this year in The Departed" (9). *Blood Diamond* provides a distinct identity even to the established actor due to the different types of roles than his former films.

The conflicting setting is the major concept in the film. The lives of individuals get threatened in such scenarios. The risky life of a journalist in a critical area is also one of the noticeable aspects of the film. The movie is also regarded as the depiction of risky journalism in the scenario of a war-torn nation, Sierra Leone Connecting with the issue of journalists in film, Alexa Milan writes in "Modern Portrayals of Journalism in Film"

REFLECTION OF HISTORY IN BLOOD DIAMOND: THE POWER OF CINEMA

The movie seems to imply that young, attractive female reporters are not afraid to use their sex appeal if it will help them land a story, a practice seen again with the character of Time magazine foreign correspondent Maddy Bowen in *Blood Diamond*. In her pursuit of a story about conflict diamonds in Sierra Leone, Maddy recognizes smuggler Danny Archer at a bar and proceeds to flirt with him. (55)

Maddy Bowen does not identify herself as a reporter until Danny realizes she is a journalist when she asks him about *Blood Diamonds*. The first few times Danny meets Maddy. They are at a bar, and she often has a beer in hand. According to Alexa Milan, it is a negative stereotypical representation of journalists. It is mentioned that Maddy Bowen asks for a strong drink, "Vodka rocks" (*Blood Diamond*).

About the female journalist Maddy Bowen, Alexa Milan further writes, "Of the three flirtatious journalists in these films, however, Maddy is perhaps the most professional. She uses her resources as a reporter to help Danny's friend, Solomon find his son, who has been forced into the military as a child soldier" (55). This reference marks that *Blood Diamond* captures multiple aspects connected with war, Violence, and poverty that occurred in the African continent realistically.

Zwick is regarded as the director who makes the cinema evoke social, cultural, and historical issues. His *The Last Samurai* evokes how the Samurai culture came to an end in Japan. About his directory venture, movie critic Richard Voeltz writes:

Edward Zwick is one of the few Hollywood directors of the past two decades whose name has come to stand not just for quality, but for a specific kind of movie: an ambitious, issue-oriented, historical epic, (*Courage under Fire. The Last Samurai*) *Blood Diamond* is very much in this tradition. Few directors give as many interviews as Edward Zwick does about his films and their meanings and messages (189).

About *Blood Diamond* Voeltz even mentions director Edward Zwick's views. According to Voeltz, the film is completely based on stone politics. Yhey views, "To me, this movie is about what is valuable. To one person, it might be a stone, to someone else, a story in a magazine, to another, it is a child. The juxtaposition of one man obsessed with finding a valuable diamond with another man risking his life to find his son is the beating heart of this film" (190).

Edward Zwick remains convinced that entertainment and ideas are not mutually exclusive in the film as Voeltz writes, "I'm more interested in those who know nothing about the subject than in preaching to the choir. How much more interesting to present a set of images to 19 year old who has never given a thought to any of this?" (190). He always tries to bring out the unknown reality through his pictures. His previous film *The Last of the Samurai* tells the story of the vanishing Samurai culture of Japan.

He, through *Blood Diamond*, aims to bring out the reality behind the chaotic situation of Sierra Leone to the world and to those who are unaware of the reality regarding Sierra Leone's politics and violence. The politics of Sierra Leone is a major issue reflected in the film. Concerning the politics behind the diamond in Sierra Leone, Rebecca Winters Keegen writing in *Time* argues:

> It is indeed hard to quantify the real impact of a film. But there are small changes wrought by recent movies, including *Blood Diamond* where the diamond industry launched a per blitz to educate consumers about conflict-free diamonds, but actually stone sales were unaffected. The movie makes advocates out of supporters. They change the world not in wide swaths of multiplexes but one popcorn bucket at a time (60)

From the above criticisms, it is clear that the film is based on the trade and smuggling of diamonds in the African context. It gives a realistic picture of Sierra Leone's politics related to diamonds and violence. The smuggling of diamonds and the consequences of violence that occurred in Sierra Leone are major concerns of the film.

Some of the critics have even focused on the Westerners' politics behind the diamond trade and the chaotic circumstance of Sierra Leone Connecting the westerner's influence in Africa as expressed in the film, Walter Rondey writes in *How Europe Underdeveloped Africa:*

> The movie is yet another depiction of the supremacy of the West. Through a tragic event in a third-world

nation, the West depicts the hegemony of the West as the messiah even at the cost of excessive damages caused by the Western capitalist. It is an irony that on the one hand, the West is responsible for culminating internal chaos, and on the other hand it acts as if applying ointment over it. (76)

According to Walter Rodney, the West is playing double roles in the entire process of getting diamonds from Sierra Leone and turning it into a war zone as well as controlling these illegal activities. This film, for him, is the medium to show the superiority of the West over the non-West.

Blood Diamond captures the involvement of teenagers and children in terror and violence as child soldiers. It is another bitter reality of conflict happening in the African continent. The beginning scene of the film gives detail regarding the violence in Sierra Leone and the involvement of child soldiers, "Dia is confused. Solomon pushes him into the hut as grinning teenage rebels appear. One wears a Tupac T-Shirt. He racks everything with AK-47 fire" (*Blood Diamond*). Thus, the film captures the realistic images of violence in Sierra Leone. The scene presents the incident of the rebel's attack on common villagers.

Thus, various critics have viewed the film from various perspectives and issues. Most of them have focused on the smuggling and trade of diamonds in Africa and Sierra Leone. This research in particular tries to focus on the representation of part of the history of Sierra Leone through new historicism. The first chapter deals with the general introduction of the topic including the reviews of literature, the second chapter includes the theoretical modality of new historicism. Similarly, the third chapter analyzes *Blood Diamond* with the new historical reading and the fourth chapter as a conclusion which concludes the film as a historical meta-fiction.

Chapter II

Historical Reflection through New Historicism
Classical History

Classical history refers to the earlier or traditional perspective on history. It marks history as the collection of factual events or incidents. Earlier traditional historians used to read literature with the base of history. They sought whether it was based on real historical events or not. They only sought an answer to what happened. What does the event tell us about history and so on? In sharp contrast to this, new historicists ask how the event has been interpreted. Traditional historians believe that history is a series of events that have a linear causal relationship.

Classical history focuses on the issue of what happened." It does not focus on how it happened. It believes in linear history and neglects the ups and downs. However, new historicists assume that history has its discontinuity; many upheavals have been left out. Old historicists like Hegel and Ranke believe that they are capable of making objective analysis but new historicists believe that one can never have objective analysis. We have our perspective of interpretation of the text. New historicists believe that we never have clear access to any basic facts of history. In this regard, Louis Tyson comments:

> The first and most important reason for this difficulty new historicist believes, is the impossibility of objective analysis. Like all human beings, historians live in a particular time and place, and their views of both current and past events are influenced

> innumerable in conscious and unconscious ways by
> their own experiences within their own culture. (279)

Every human being lives in a certain time and place. Their consciousness is shaped by society, the state, and their socioeconomic status. Our views regarding past and present are shaped by our culture and society. Classical history is always contaminated, oblique, and subjective. Classical history itself claims as the collection of truth and facts. Similarly, it tries to place itself in a different position than literary writing. However, there are many loopholes in classical history.

Classical History: Pros and Cons

Michel Foucault, a radical poststructuralist thinker came up with his new idea about "discourse", 'power', 'truth', and 'representation' to show the loopholes inherent within classical history. He questions the truth that history claims and said truths are created by making discourses, which are made through knowledge. For him, power is a matter of representation. Through representation, power is created and through power, the subject is created with distorted representation. So, these key terms create a cycle that is durable for sometimes until power has been transformed into another system.

A network of power, truth, and discourse empowers certain institutions that subjugate or encircle other powerless institutions that are represented according to the desires of the so-called power-having institutions with certain distorted images. So, power-having institutions exercise power by creating a discourse with domineering ideologies that even enhance to formulate 'truth' to dominate or marginalize other institutions.

He opines that discourses are rooted in social institutions and that social and political power operates through discourse. The oppositional nature of new historicism subverts earlier monopolized tendencies of the works and certain institutions.

So, Foucault attempts to negate official history because it documents information in linear order by sidelining other hidden information that later may become the core medium to expose the politics of official history. Opposing official history Foucault argues, "Effective history, however, deals with events in terms of their most unique characteristics, their most acute manifestations" (94). In his first volume of *History of Sexuality*, he claims, "Power is everywhere [...] power comes from below; that is there is no binary and all-encompassing opposition between ruler and ruled at the root of power relations and serving as a general matrix." (93-4). He assumes that power is not the force of prohibition rather it has a productive native nature. It traverses and produces things, and induces pleasure, forms, knowledge, and discourse.

Michel Foucault does not believe in the linear study of history and says that history does not have objectivity. Therefore, he proposes a genealogical study of history to unearth significant facts, making history complete, and meaningful while rejecting archeological history. For him " History is the concrete body of development with its moments of intensity, its lapses, its extended period of feverish agitation, its fainting spells; and only a metaphysician would seek its soul in the distant ideality of the origin" (85-86).

Michel Foucault is always aware of the fact that a historian cannot escape the 'situatedness' of one's time and space. He takes historians as 'embedded' in his social practices. Through this, it is clear that history is written from the perspective of the historian. The position, a historian occupies in society determines the history of who writes. Foucault in his essay " Nietzsche, Geneology and History" states that 'devotion to truth and the precision of scientific methods arose from the passion of scholars, their reciprocal hatred, their fanatical and unending discussion, and their spirit of competition, their conflicts that slowly forged the weapons of reason" (83-84). He criticizes the traditional history that seeks the lofty origin which is a metaphysical extension that arises from the belief that things are most precious and essential at the moment of birth.

Michael Foucault's "Truth and Power" posits the view of discontinuity in history. Disregarding the structuralists' systematic effort to evaluate the concept of the event not only from ethnology and other sciences especially from history he leads to the susceptible analysis of history. He further states, "It's not a matter of locating everything on one level, that of the event but of realizing that there is actually a whole order of levels of different types of events differing in amplitude chronological breadth and capacity to produce effects" (1137).

Now it becomes clear that Michel Foucault argues for the historical contextualization of the text to get its meaning. He says, "Historical contextualization needed to be something more than the simple relativization of the phenomenological subject. [...] The problem can be solved by historicizing the subject as posited by the phenomenologist, fabricating a subject that evolves through the course of history" (1138). He becomes traditional historians' pains take to be objective but ultimately they have shaped thought in a particular time and place. Effective history takes knowledge as perspective. He further states, "Historians take unusual pains to erase the elements in their work which reveal their grounding in a particular time and place, their preferences in a controversy is an avoidable obstacle of their passion" (96).

According to Foucault, historians take themselves as superior beings and do not allow others to stand above them. He further says, "The objectivity of historians inverts the relationships of will and knowledge and it is in the same stroke, a necessary belief in providence, in final causes and teleology—the beliefs that place the historian in the family of ascetics" (97). Most interesting idea with genealogy is its scope. Firstly, genealogy attacks the supposed coherence of thinking "subject'; it dissolves the function of singular human identity. Thirdly, it attacks the notion of origin in historical investigations. Fourthly, genealogy stresses the idea of history as discontinuity. Finally, it focuses not upon ideas or historical mentalities but upon the 'body' to show it is imprinted by 'history'.

Foucault criticizes the traditional method of writing history which reconstructs a comprehensive view of history and retraces the past as a patient and continuous development. Those devices must be systematically dismantled and dismissed. He suggests his type of history, i.e. effective history as he further clarifies:

> History becomes "effective" to the degree that it introduces a discontinuity into our very being- as it divides our emotions, dramatizes our instincts, multiplies our body, and sets it against itself. "Effective" history deprives the self of the reassuring

stability of life and nature, and it will not permit itself to be transported by a voiceless obstinacy toward a millennial ending. It will uproot its traditional foundations and restlessly disrupt its pretended continuity. (93)

Thus, based on Foucault's idea regarding the analysis of historiography it can be said that he is in favor of effective history, i.e. genealogical approach to history which explains the loopholes of history, and observes the suffering of repressed, dominated, and marginalized people. His radical views about reality, identity, history, truth, and knowledge have given sufficient impetus to new historicism to rethink these ideas and make the contextual study of the text to get meaning of the text.

Friedrich Nietzsche, the pioneer of deconstruction, questions the relation of language to truth. According to him language never expresses truth. Language is used by human beings to create the so-called truth for their survival but it fails to capture the real essence. He opines that one should suspend the assumption that language has the truth. The use of language is guided by the 'will to power'. Nietzsche further states, "Truth is a mobile army of metaphors, metonymy, and morphemes" (636). Histories too are guided by constructed truths, by power and the fictions too are not merely a fantasy or imagination, rather there is the influence of fact incidents of historical timeframe.

Truth itself is the product of relations of power and of the systems in which it follows; it changes as the system changes as Michel Foucault states:

Truth is a thing of this world; it is produced only by virtue of multiple forms of constraint. And it induces regular effects of power. Each society has its regime of truth, its 'general politics' of truth: that is, the types of discourse that it accepts and makes function as true. (qtd. in Adams 1144)

Power is generated in society by producing discourse and by constructing truths. Power determines the truth and as soon as the system of society changes truth also changes. Foucault further states that "Truth is the sort of error that cannot be refuted because it was hardened into an unalterable in the long baking process of history" (85). For Nietzsche, "Only by means of forgetfulness can man ever arrive at imagining that he possesses truth" (635). However, there are illusions instead of truth. Truth is the illusion of which one has forgotten to be so. In this regard, Stephen Greenblatt says, "Truth itself is radically unstable and yet constantly stabilized" (74). In this sense, the 'truth' raised by traditional history is questioned by New Historicists.

New Historicism and its Rationale

New historicism, which emerged in the early 1980s, opposes Formalism and New Criticism's focus on the text as an autonomous entity. Stephen Greenblatt's *Renaissance Self-Fashioning from More to Shakespeare* (1980) is usually regarded as the first book from which new Historicism was developed as a mode of literary theory. New historicism is a method based on the parallel reading of literary and non-literary work, usually of the same historical era. Stephen Greenblatt,

REFLECTION OF HISTORY IN BLOOD DIAMOND: THE POWER OF CINEMA

Louis Montrose, and H. Aram Veseer are some of the prominent new historicists.

According to new Historicists, every literary text has its situation within the institutions, social practices, and discourses that constitute the overall culture of a particular time and place. In this regard, Louis Montrose takes new historicism as a shift from an essential or immanent to a historical, contextual, and conjunctural model of signification and a general suspicion of closed systems, totalities, and universals (393).

The assumption such as neutrality of language, absence of domineering ideologies, and narrating voices are questioned by New Historicism. The concepts, themes, and procedures of new historicist criticism took shape in the late 1970s especially in the writings of Michel Foucault and the early 1980s, most prominently written by scholars of the English Renaissance. It primarily focuses on the historical, cultural, economic, and political conditions of the production of the text, its meaning, and its effects. No text can be put in isolation from its historical context. It is impossible to get objective truth in any text because like all human beings and writers also live in a particular time and place and their views are shaped consciously or unconsciously by the experiences within their own culture Louis Montrose defines the new historicism "as a reciprocal concern with the historicity of texts and textuality of history" (416).

New historicism and cultural criticism share a significant theoretical common ground, both emphasizing the historical context, including the social, cultural, and economic milieu of text production. Cultural criticism cannot be easily separated from new historicism. These theories directly oppose structuralist and new critical assumptions about objectivity, timelessness, and autonomous verbal objects. In the preface of *The New Historicism Reader,* H. Aram Veeser writes that New Historicism assumes:

> 1) That every expressive act is embedded in a network of material practices; 2) that every act of unmasking, critique, and opposing uses the tools it condemns and risks falling prey to the practice it exposes; 3) that literary and non-literary" texts" circulate inseparably; 4) that no discourse, imaginative or archival, gives access to unchanging truths or expresses unalterable human nature; and 5) that a critical method and a language adequate to describe culture under capitalism participate in the economy they describe. (2)

These assumptions can be taken as some of the basic tenets of new historicism. History generally refers to the past events that have been recorded in various forms such as a book, film, text, and so on. Traditional historians supposed history as an objective or pure history but new historicists have brought new concepts of history. They take historical accounts as narratives or stories that are inevitably biased according to the point of view, conscious or unconscious of those who wrote them.

Stephen Greenblatt, one of the famous theorists of new historicism published *Renaissance Self-Fashioning* which is taken as the milestone book for establishing the trend of the new historical study of the text. In his essay "Towards a Poetics of Culture" he defines new historicism as "a practice rather than doctrine, since as far as I can tell (I should be the one to know)

REFLECTION OF HISTORY IN BLOOD DIAMOND: THE POWER OF CINEMA

its no doctrine at all" (1). Greenblatt's detailed and perspective analysis emphasizes that is informed by the same cultural dialectic as society at large. A text reflects as well as supports its dialectic, or to put it differently, a socio-historical context conditions its textual representations and likewise, a text informs and sometimes even conditions the historical process.

Similarly, Greenblatt refutes any form of essentialist humanism which regards man as an autonomous, free, transcendental essence. In this regard, in the essay entitled "The New Historicism of Stephen Greenblatt: On Poetics of Culture and the Interpretation of Shakespeare" Jan R. Veenstra states, "This is one of the two major presuppositions that are recognized as essential to the movement. The second is that the historian or critic is the product of his or her historical moment and only capable of knowing historical alterity through the framework of the present" (3).

In his essay "The Improvisation of Power" Greenblatt opines his view on how power shapes all literary texts. The term improvisation means "the ability both to capitalize on the unforeseen and to transform given materials into one's own scenario" (50), Greenblatt opines that every text has its own motive to exercise power which is circulated through the construction of discourse(s). No, any text is separate from subjectivity, time, and place. He further says "Violence, sexual anxiety, and improvisation are the materials out of which the drama is constructed" (54).

He takes improvisation as a central Renaissance mode of behavior. In the sixteenth century, Western Europe increasingly established its ownership of labor and resources of those who were at the marginal periphery. In this context, he takes the help of Shakespeare's drama *Othello* and remarks: "Iago is fully aware of himself as an improviser and reveals in his ability to manipulate his victims, to lead them by the nose like asses, to possess their labor with their ever being capable of grasping the relation in which they are enmeshed" (55).

Stephen Orgel in his essay "The Role of King" examines that roles in plays are deliberately deceiving and all of them are lies. For him "A government's power depends on its ability to enforce its authority" (41). He assumes that authors give roles to characters according to their choice. They present their characters from their point of view not from the audience. Therefore, observers take roles as deceiving and fooling. Authors show their characters as what the audience wants to be and not the way others see them.

Greenblatt in his essay "The Improvisation of Power" notices Iago's racist attitude toward Othello through a new historicist's perspective. Despite his being junior to Othello, Iago succeeds in the conspiracy. In this context, Greenblatt opines, "Though he finds himself in a subordinate position, the ensign regards his black general as 'an erring barbarian' whose 'free and open nature' is a fertile field for exploitation" (56). For him, "Iago must ultimately destroy the beings he exploits and hence undermines the profitable economy of his own relations but that destruction may be long deferred, deferred in fact for precisely the length of the play" (56). Being in a submissive role, Iago weaves the net of conspiracy easily. His subordinate position helps to hide his villainous intention. Nobody suspects him. He takes advantage of Othello's simplicity and gullibility. Iago ultimately destroys Othello's happy family life. Now it becomes clear that Iago has done conspiracy to destroy Othello" and Desdemona to fulfill his desire. Though his intention is clear from the middle part of the play he becomes successful at the last part of the play.

Thus, Stephan Greenblatt dubbed 'new historicism' from an older, reflections, and positivist literary historical scholarship and from New Critical formalism. It utterly rejects the old historicists' distinction between "literature' and 'history', between 'text' and 'context'. It also resists the idea of the autonomous individual. No author or work can be set against a social or literary background. In this context, Greenblatt comments, "The contours of art and literature are socially and historically configured: distinctions between artistic production and other kinds of social production. [...] are not intrinsic to the texts; rather they are made up and constantly redrawn by artists, audiences, and readers" (398).

No doubt every text is shaped by historical and social factors of our society the time of its production and the writer's individuality. The author's individuality is also shaped by the time and social, cultural, economic, and political situations in which the literary figure is living. Regarding autonomy in his introduction to *Renaissance Self- Fashioning* Greenblatt writes, "That family, state and religious institutions impose a more rigid and far-reaching discipline upon their middle-class and aristocratic subjects... the central issue the power to impose a shape upon oneself is an aspect of the more general power to control identity (1)

There is not a single self but multiple selves. Renaissance authors always tried to fashion their selves in their works of art. These selves- a sense of personal order, a characteristic mode of address to the world, and a structure of bounded desires are always shaping the expression of identity and its formation.

Human beings are not free from culture. Culture means not only complexes of concrete behavior, patterns such as customer usage, tradition, and so on. However, culture encompasses a set of control mechanisms such as; plans, recipes, rules, and instructions for the governing of behavior. In this context, Greenblatt states, "Literature functions within this system in three interlocking ways: as a manifestation of the concrete behavior of its particular authors, as itself the expression of the codes by which behavior is shaped, and as a reflection upon those codes" (4).

He assumes that interpretation without these three ways becomes imperfect so the literary text should be examined through different perspectives. If literature is seen only as a detached reflection upon the prevailing behavioral codes it leads back toward a conception of art as addressed to a timeless, cultureless, universal human essence or as a self-regarding, autonomous entity. Particular cultures and the observers of these cultures are inevitably drawn to a metaphorical grasp of reality.

Artistic representation cannot be a distinct human activity. It has some affinities to the given culture, its proper goal, and history. Authors cannot be separated from the texts they create because they constantly return to particular lives and particular situations, to the material necessities and social pressure that men and women daily confront with. Greenblatt also writes about the power that at once localized in a particular institution—court, the church, the colonial administration- diffuses in ideological structure of meaning that characterizes modes of expression and recurrent narrative patterns. He further states, "Art does not pretend to be autonomy: the written word is self-consciously embedded in specific communities, life situations, and structures of power" (7). Power changes in different ways and so do the forms of discourses. It shifted from the church to the book to the absolutist state and from celebration to rebellion, to subversive submission in Renaissance Period. He writes, "Self-fashioning occurred at the point of encounter between an authority and an alien that what is marked for attack and hence that any achieved identity always contains within itself the signs of its own subversion or loss" (9).

Louis Montrose, a leading new historicist, views literature and history as interdependent. New historicism reconfigures the relationship between the verbal and the social, between the text and the context. It rejects some prevalent alternative idealist, empiricist, and materialist conceptions of literature as an autonomous aesthetic, moral, or intellectual order. Montrose comments that "Writing and reading are always historically and socially situated events, performed in the world and upon the world by ideologically situated individual and collective human agents" (415). Montrose emphasizes that authors represent the characters, world, and subject matter or create discourses according to their position where they inhabit:

> Representations of the world in written discourse participate in the construction of the world; they are engaged in shaping the modalities of social reality and in accommodating their writers, performers, readers, and audiences to multiple and shifting subject positions within the world that they both constitute and inhabit. (396)

Montrose believes that a closed and static monolithic and homogeneous notion of ideology must be replaced by heterogeneous and unstable permeable and procedural. Proper attention must be given to the manifold meditations involved in the production, reproduction, and appropriation of ideological dominance. He further claims, "All texts are ideologically marked, however multivalent or inconsistent that inscription may be" (405).

New Historical Reading of Literary Work

The 'historicity of texts' means that the text is embedded with certain economic, cultural, social, and political conditions of its production. The mode of reading is also determined by the cultural, political, social, and economic embeddedness of the readers. In the same way 'textuality of history' means that history cannot be purely objective. Objectivity is determined by power and culture as Louis Tyson says "Our subjectivity or selfhood is shaped by and shapes the culture into which we were born" (280).

As told by Peter Barry, the text has a certain historical quality because it is situated within a certain historical timeframe and influenced by current social and political reality, the film *Blood Diamond* has some sort of historical reality. It captures the chaotic and conflicting issue of violence in the Sierra Leone Civil War in 1996-2001. Furthermore, all the events and incidents are directly associated with the part of the history of Sierra Leone. The events like Westerners' extreme greed for diamonds, the interest in diamonds which creates various terrorist groups according to the design of international smugglers, the struggle between government loyalists and insurgent forces as well as the representation of various worldwide conferences regarding issues of African struggles, issue of diamonds, the refugee of Sierra Leone, etc., are some historical facts reflected in the film. In this sense, the history and text cannot be separated like *Blood Diamond* and the official history of Sierra Leone during the last decade of the 20th century as H. Aram Vesser comments, "Literary and non-literary texts circulate inseparably. History and literature have been endlessly juxtaposed before now, but never in quite so insouciant fashion" (16).

Chapter III

Reflection of History in *Blood Diamond*

Based on Sierra Leone's history during the last decade of the 20th century, the film *Blood Diamond* captures the social-political reality as if history in fictional form. Being a political war thriller, the film captures Sierra Leone's civil war from 1996 to 2001 including the social and political realities of Sierra Leone; politics behind the rich minerals like diamonds, the civil war between the government and other terrorist groups, and the interfere of various foreign trade groups. In this sense, the film stands as the true reflection of the critical violent circumstances of Sierra Leone and the unhealthy power practice and struggle for diamonds according to the interests and greed of various political/non-political groups, western smugglers, and tradesmen.

Blood Diamond not only represents the true history of Sierra Leone in realistic representation but also depicts how the African countries are torn apart by violence and struggles and most of the natives have been living the lives of refugees and exiled due to the greed of the treasures and valuable minerals like diamonds. Most of the characters in the film go through the plights and consequences related to the diamond smuggling and terrorism in the nation which is not beyond the historical facts of Sierra Leone. The suffering of the characters associated with Sierra Leone's political situation directly presupposes that the film is a historical representation of a particular time frame of the society and nation.

Reflection of RUF Terror and Conflict

REFLECTION OF HISTORY IN BLOOD DIAMOND: THE POWER OF CINEMA

At the beginning of the film, the words appear, "Sierra Leone 1999" (*Blood Diamond*) which indicates that it deals with the location of Sierra Leone and captures the time frame of the last decade of the 20th century. The information is followed by audiences to mark the time and locality which presupposes that the film is somehow related to the certain history of the nation. Then, in the first scene of the film, the major character, Solomon is introduced with his family members. Through his rough hands, the director establishes him as a hard-working common person of Sierra Leone. Solomon, the hard-working native talks with his son and provides the detail that he aims to make his son a doctor in the future.

The first scene of the film captures the reality of Solomon's family. He is a hardworking working class person and optimistic for his son's future. Similarly, the scene provides the identity of other family members including Solomon's wife, a younger daughter of twelve years old, and an infant brother. Throughout the scene, the director introduces the lower-class working people or native villagers as the primary focus of the film. It gives a picture of the harmonious and optimistic lives of common villagers in Sierra Leone.

Drastically, the director changes the scene from this peaceful lower-class family environment to a horrific circumstance. Solomon's hut and even the entire village face the sudden and unexpected attack by other people with weapons. The attackers are similar to Solomon since all are from native communities and similar socio-political backgrounds. Only the difference is that the attackers are present brutally and most of the members of this terrorist group are teenagers with heavy machinery weapons like guns and weapons. The terrorist group was introduced as the Revolutionary United Front (RUF). The film presents the scene of attacking the village as Solomon says to his wife and children "Go back inside...now" (*Blood Diamond*) terrified of the attack. The chaotic situation of the village attack is presented further as:

> Dia is confused. Solomon pushes him into the hut as grinning teenage rebels appear. One wears a Tupac T-shirt. He racks everything with AK-47 fire. Huts. Animals. People. Solomon dives to the ground. Villagers run screaming. Chickens squawk, oxen bray. Two mud- splattered PICK-UP TRUCKS with sawed-off roofs crash through the bush, full of R. U. F. REBELS, who quickly jump off... shouting, wielding machetes and automatic rifles, BANDOLIERS of AMMO crisis-crossed on their bare chests, GRENADES on their belts. (*Blood Diamond*)

The reference from the script gives detailed information about the nature of the attack and the attackers. It is the RUF who attacks Solomon's village. Most of the rebels are teenage boys with AK-47s in their hands and grenades on their belts.

The picture of terrible violence is reflected when the operation of rebels against the villagers comes on screen. All these appear from the perspective of Solomon as "Solomon cowers admit the gunfire, looks around frantically. Men and boys are being mended up. Huts set on fire. Suddenly he is yanked up as two rebels pull him away" (*Blood Diamond*). Thus, Solomon is captured by the rebels but his other family members can escape,

"Jessie exists in their hut, infant in her arms, mad with fear" (*Blood Diamond*). Jessie calls Solomon but Solomon only utters the word "Run" (*Blood Diamond*) to make them escape from the attack.

The attack on the entire village by the gun holders, randomly killing innocent people provides realistic pictures of the violence and civil war of Sierra Leone. All the captured people of the village are placed in line waiting for death, to cut hands, or to be herded for work. The situation is presented as:

> REBELS prod them with rifles, making them from a line. All under the watchful sunglasses of an R. U. F. COLONEL. The first villager is shoved to his knees in front of a tree stump. A muscle-bound, SHIRTLESS REBEL with a gleaming AXE strut over, his eyes glazed from palm wine and marijuana. A second rebel grabs the village man's hand and places it on the stump. The man pulls his hand away. Tupac T-Shirt puts the AK-47 in his hand. The choice is clear. Your hand or your head. The villager tries to scramble away. RAT-A- TAT! Bullet through his hand. (*Blood Diamond*)

The scene captures the killing and cutting of the hands of innocent villagers by the RUF. Most of the villagers who are unable to work are killed. For the physically strong men, they take for work in diamond mining. It is presented as, "The next in the line, A STRONG YOUNG MAN, is pushed to the stump" (*Blood Diamond*) and the RUF. Colonel says, "Not him. He can work" (*Blood Diamond*) and he is herded into a waiting truck.

Most of the people are killed and some of their hands are cut. Their hands are cut so they cannot vote in the forthcoming national election. In this connection the Colonel of RUF says, "No hands. No votes, R. U. F. is coming" (*Blood Diamond*). Among the victims of such criminal acts, there are basically incapable people to work. The scene is well captured in the film while Solomon is in line to get his hand cut, it is clear that capable people are sent for laborious work for the terrorist group like searching for diamonds. Solomon's laborious and harsh hands make sure to the team leader of the terrorist group that he can work hard and find diamonds for them. In this connection the team leader says, "You will need your hand" (*Blood Diamond*), and like the previous young man Solomon too is herded to the waiting truck. Then, Solomon is imprisoned for the hard labor of searching for diamonds for the terrorist group. Now the film centers on the politics behind diamond and its consequence of violence, terror, and exile of thousands of Sierra Leoneans. Solomon's family members like other thousands are obliged to go to refugee camps.

The attacks of terrorists, mass killing, burning of villages, and forcing people to work for the group, etc., are some of the realistic pictures of Sierra Leone during the last decade of the 20th century. Furthermore, it truly refers to the terrorist group as the Revolutionary United Front (RUF). The RUF was the real terrorist group of contemporary Sierra Leone and they used child soldiers as well as attacked common villagers which all are not beyond the realities of Sierra Leone. Similarly, the major cause behind such consequences is the rich minerals like diamonds and outsiders' interest in them. The use of forced labor by RUF in search of diamonds too is not beyond the historical reality of contemporary Sierra Leone society. The incidents that occurred in the film truthfully refer to the historical facts of Sierra Leone.

Diamond as the Major Cause of Conflict

Diamond is the major cause of the conflict in Sierra Leone from the beginning. The conflict in Sierra Leone begins through the direct sponsorship of diamond bandits who then smuggle the gems through the border of Sierra Leone. This version of the origin of the conflict peaks while the RUF and later two military juntas, the National Provisional Ruling Council and the Armed Forces Revolutionary Council, all shared a similar ideological stance on diamond smuggling. The political conflict in Sierra Leone too has its own, independent origins, which was rooted in the conflict through smuggling diamonds through Liberia.

The major cause of conflict in Sierra Leone is the diamonds of its nation. Diamond is taken by such rebel groups and sold to other Western trade groups. The film not only captures the issues happening within Sierra Leone but also presents the greed of Westerners toward diamonds. After being captured by RUF Solomon searches for diamonds for RUF and at the same time an International G8 Conference is presented in the film which tries to address the issue of illegal diamond supply of Sierra Leone as the conference is marked "G8 Conference on Diamonds Antwerp, Belgium" (*Blood Diamond*). In this conference, the participant addresses:

> Throughout the history of Africa... whenever a substance of value is found... the locals die in great

numbers and misery... Now, this was true of ivory, rubber, gold, and oil. It is now true of diamonds. According to a devastating report by Global Witness... these stones are being used to purchase arms and finance civil war. We must act to prohibit... the direct or indirect import of all rough diamonds from conflict zones. May I remind you? The USA is responsible for two-thirds of all diamond purchases worldwide... I don't anticipate that demand diminishing (*Blood Diamond*)

The G8 conference, visualized in film, captures the true essence of Sierra Leone's history during the conflict. It presents the reality that the legal or illegal supply of diamonds has contributed to the purchase of weapons and increased violence in Sierra Leone. It is quite justifiable and the film too is centered on the relationship between diamonds and conflict.

The title *Blood Diamond* captures the association of violence with diamonds. Each scene of the film is thematically associated with the issues of Sierra Leone. While Solomon is searching for diamonds in minerals, one of the forced laborers hides a diamond in his mouth. Subsequently, he is shot on the spot seizing his diamond. The incident occurs just before Solomon finds another large-sized pink diamond and he hides it in his toe. Most of the time diamonds are presented with blood. While Archer is smuggling diamonds through Sierra Leone and Liberia's border, the diamonds are brought out from goats' bodies and washed with blood. The diamond found by Solomon is the major turning point of the film which is a little larger and pink in color. The blood-painted diamond symbolically refers to the terrorism and violence of Sierra Leone due to the diamonds.

In Sierra Leone, during the civil war, the property rights regime over diamonds was weak enough that rebels from the Revolutionary United Front (RUF) were able to seize control of the diamond mining region almost immediately after the groups' inception as a violent movement. These already inadequate property rights were thoroughly disrupted throughout the decade-long war, with the RUF, the government-backed and later rebellious military, and South African Executive Outcomes mercenaries instituting new property rights at the point of a gun. There are many constraints on the government of Sierra Leone in the use of its natural resources resulting, for instance, from the practice of mortgaging rights to diamond mining to pay for the war. There is a post-conflict opportunity to take a critical look at the governance of natural resources and include innovative approaches to their use in plans to improve income generation, social and economic development, and participation in the international economic system.

There is the role of foreign tradesmen especially Euro-Americans behind the critical situation of Sierra Leone. Even the RUF Colonel pours his agony on white masters who are the cause of terrorism. He says, "The violent situation is the result of the greed of Westerners" (*Blood Diamond*). Thus, it is clear that the connection between diamond politics and terror in Sierra Leone during the rise of RUF in the film *Blood Diamond* is a perfect example of a reflection of Sierra Leone's part of history through visual representation in fictional form. The horrific picture of

Sierra Leone that it has been turning to be a critical war zone due to the unequal power relation between Western nations and Africa as well as due to the greed of Westerners for the valuable minerals of Sierra Leone is expressed in film through the arrival of Danny Archer (Leonardo DiCaprio). Just before the scene, Solomon finds the pink colored diamond, Archer appears in the scene, with the team leader of rebels and he makes an agreement with the rebel commander and takes the diamonds. The scene justifies that he purchases diamonds with weapons for the rebels to wrestle against the government forces. The scene presupposes that the smugglers of diamonds have a relationship with rebellious groups.

The smugglers not only have a relationship with rebel groups but also with the governmental forces. Archer smuggles the diamonds to Liberia with the support and commission of government armies. The critical conflict zone is the borderline of Sierra Leone and Liberia regarding the smuggling of diamonds as Iryna Marchuk writes, "Beyond the neighboring country of Liberia, there is still a border international link in the beginnings of the Sierra Leonean conflict" (89), Archer's smuggling of diamond on the way to Liberia to is not untouched with the social reality of diamond smuggling of Sierra Leone. The scene captures the bitter reality of Sierra Leone and how the country has been turning to a critical location due to the play of Western tradesmen and companies who use both governmental and rebellious groups in order to fulfill their greed. The commoners like Solomon should be the scapegoat in such a situation.

While Archer is smuggling diamonds, Solomon, on the other hand, is searching for diamonds for RUF. All his family members are going on the way to the refugee camp. Solomon luckily finds a large pink-colored diamond and hides in the forests but he is caught by a rebel Colonel suddenly government armies attack them and they are sent to jail. In jail, the colonel finds Solomon and asks for the diamond. The story of this pink-colored diamond leads to the kidnapping of Solomon's son who is going to a refugee camp with his mother and is recruited to RUF. While Solomon is searching for his family members in the refugees list his son Dia is shown captured by the group of child soldiers of RUF.

Use of Child Military Force

The pathetic situation of children's use in terrorist activities in Sierra Leone is reflected in the film with the scene of Dia with other child soldiers. The Colonel of RUF makes Dia unknowingly kill a man with the gun and declares him the captain. The scene captures the manipulation and brainwashing of children to use them in criminal activities. To motivate the children for terrorist activities, the Colonel says:

> Your fathers and mothers are dead. Your brothers and sisters are dead. You are dead. You have been reborn. We are your family now. Your parents are weak. They're the farmers. They're the fishermen. They've done nothing but suck the blood from this country. But you are the heroes who will have this nation. You're men. You are not children anymore. (*Blood Diamond*)

In this way, the Colonel of RUF manipulates the children to be involved in terrorist activities as RUF soldiers. The Colonel focuses on Dia basically because he aims to bargain with

Solomon for the diamond he has found. Furthermore, the Colonel motivates the children, "No one has ever given you respect. But with this (Machine gun) in your hands, they go fear you. If you do not get the respect you deserve" (*Blood Diamond*).

The forceful recruitment of children as RUF is the true historical incident of Sierra Leone. The forceful use of male labor in the search for diamonds and girls' use for sexual and domestic labor are facts associated with Sierra Leone's history during 1990-2001. The civil war or the conflict in Sierra Leone was started in 1990-1991 as Paul Richards writes, "...when Foday Sankoh, a charismatic former military corporal, hijacked an unorganized movement of young boys who were gathering in Freetown after the institution of fees for government schools" (8).

In this sense, the use of child soldiers too is the fact associated with Sierra Leone's part of history. Paul Richards further mentions, "From this initial group of boys, Sankoh built an army largely made of children, with both boys and girls being used as fighters. Girls were also used for sexual and domestic labor" (9). The recruitment methods of the RUF included; threatening children and teenagers that if they did not join the rebels, their families would be murdered in front of them, often following rape and torture which is presented in *Blood Diamond*. The beginning two scenes visualize the RUF system of recruitment procedures for child soldiers, their manipulation, and their use in terrorist activities. Similarly, through Solomon's son, Dia, the clear picture of using children in the military field in Sierra Leone is shown.

REFLECTION OF HISTORY IN BLOOD DIAMOND: THE POWER OF CINEMA

Blood Diamond presents live-action scenes while presenting child soldiers. In one of these segments, the audience is brought into the rebel camp. Child soldiers cavort across a concrete slab with makeshift canvas tents and metal scaffolding. One child swings back and forth on a rope through the center of the stage as others engage in drinking, dancing, and smoking. Most wear hats of varying types including berets, visors, and a knit hat with a giant pom-pom, and many hold weapons. In another frame, the camera zooms in on a man wearing a sleeveless leather jacket and cowry bracelet before panning out to reveal Dia, He is situated on a couch next to Commander Rambo, whose eyes are shaded behind red sunglasses. As he injects drugs into Dia's arm, Rambo tells the boy, "The medicine will make you strong and make you invisible to enemies. Bullets will bounce off you" (*Blood Diamond*). This statement should recall the use of amulets employed for similar purposes. Drug usage resonates across narratives of the child soldier.

Regarding the use of child labor and their manipulation, Paul Richards mentions, "The R. U. F. has been accused of forcing these children to be injected with cocaine as well as to eat gunpowder as part of ongoing indoctrination rituals" (10). Once children were indoctrinated into the RUF, they were often forced to lead raids against their own villages as tests of their loyalty. At the beginning of the film Solomon's village too attacked by similar child soldiers under the leadership of the RUF leader.

In *Blood Diamond*, even the girls are used as the military force by RUF. Regarding the use of women or girls both as a military force and in sexual violence, Chris Coulter writes, "Women have been targeted systematically with sexual violence.

But there have been women fighters as well, particularly amongst the RUF" (11). While causing an extraordinary exclusion from all kinds of basic needs and frequent submission to human rights violations. The film even captures the bitter reality of Sierra Leone's history during the civil war.

In the history of Sierra Leone, the long-experienced generational power gap became questioned when young fighters challenged the chiefs and set up their local governance structures. There are several reasons to explain the war, its outbreak, and its prolongation. An emerging consensus suggests that the root cause lies in the weakness, injustice, and rampant corruption within both local and national governments. Although external factors, such as the supply of revolutionary ideology and training by Libya or logistic support from Liberia and Burkina Faso, etc., have been necessary ingredients to kick-start and maintain the war, they are in themselves insufficient explanation. Alluvial diamonds-dubbed 'lootable resources", because they can be extracted without significant investment in machinery - have nurtured the war once it had begun and had stabilized it on a highly violent level, leaving previous political motivations often aside.

In this sense, the social-political reality of Sierra Leone during the time of 1991- 2001 is visually represented in *Blood Diamond* as if the film is a living history of contemporary Sierra Leone. An adventure story set in Sierra Leone during the civil wars of the 1990s by portraying gut-wrenching violence and bloodshed, including issues like; child soldiers, conflict diamonds, and the complicity of the diamond monopoly makes the movie a part of Sierra Leone's history.

REFLECTION OF HISTORY IN BLOOD DIAMOND: THE POWER OF CINEMA

Similarly, the replacement of the people to refugees is clear in the film as Solomon's family and villagers are obliged to be internal refugees inside their homeland. Regarding the pitiful history of Sierra Leone during the civil war Danny Hoffman writes:

> The civil war in Sierra Leone inflicted tremendous human suffering on the population. The death toll in the war is probably close to 75,000, 2 million persons have been displaced and 20,000 mutilated. The war increased morbidity and mortality rates, particularly amongst the most vulnerable rural poor. The actual battlefield death is minor in comparison to the burden inflicted by war-related malnutrition and the collapse of health services. It is, however, difficult to identify particular victims of this war: no specific ethnic group was targeted, and no horizontal inequalities were exploited to fuel the war. (105)

The war has caused a tremendous refugee crisis and internal displacement. It is realistically presented in *Blood Diamond* It reflects the internally displaced persons during the terrific village attack by RUF.

The film captures the reality of people's replacement as refugees through its scene at the Guinea Refugee Camp. According to the war report, it is estimated that more than two-thirds of the population was displaced internally. In the film when Solomon visits the refugee camp to find his family, the large numbers of displaced people appear in the scene.

Roles of Foreign Companies for Conflict in Sierra Leone

Behind the pitiful situation of civil war and the suffering of Sierra Leone's people, there is a direct or indirect role of foreign tradesmen and companies. The violence in Sierra Leone is directly linked to its natural resources of diamonds. The involvement of international mafias in the smuggling and trade of diamonds has caused conflict in Sierra Leone. Danny Archer, in *Blood Diamond*, is used by similar diamond mafias. Here, the Colonel of the army himself is presented as one of the involved mafias. Danny Archer becomes just a puppet because he is forced by Colonel Coetzee to find and bring a diamond for him. In the scene, at Cape Town in South Africa, the meeting of Coetzee and Archer reveals the reality through the conservation between them:

"And you survived. A log of boys didn't. Why is that?"

"Just Lucky, I guess,"

"No, you were a good soldier. But I made you better, didn't I?"

"Yes Sir, You did."

"And over the years I didn't protect you, teach you about diamonds, cut you in on the deals? So might call it that, yeah-but not you because you done with me now, eh? On to bigger things. I need a man that knows his way around up there. Unless, of course, you wanna cut me in. Something pink?"

"Sir."

"Our deal went band, and you owe money, I'll take the stone as payment." (*Blood Diamond*)

The conversation between Archer and Colonel Coetzee reveals the greed of the foreign army that is sent to establish peace and order in Sierra Leone. These types of foreign organizations and so-called human activists in the name of maintaining peace, have been working in their favor. Colonel Coetzee's greed for diamonds further leads the film to a critical situation since he too runs after the pink diamond found by Solomon.

The dual nature of the so-called foreign peacemaker in Sierra Leone is also brought to light. Colonel Coetzee on the one hand has come to Sierra Leone to take the rebels down. Their military has this agreement with the government of Sierra Leone. On the other hand, the Colonel has been supplying weapons for the rebel groups because of how much the political situation becomes critical so much the chances to fulfill his greed. The dual nature of the Colonel is revealed through the conversation between Danny Archer and the Colonel:

'It seems the rebels have taken back the diamond fields, Danny. The government of Sierra Leone has contracted us to go there and take the rebels down.

'So you sell the rebels weapons, the government hires you when they

use them? Nice sir."

We save the government they show their gratitude."

And you get rich. Right?' (*Blood Diamond*)

The conversation reveals the fact that the same institutions have been supplying weapons for the rebels and have been so-called help to the government to calm rebels down. These types of acts of foreign greedy organizations for diamonds have been turning Sierra Leone into a play zone of war. The act is leading innocent people to extreme suffering and miseries, Solomon and his family members have been scapegoats in the critical situation of Sierra Leone.

Blood Diamond depicts the actual political and social reality of Sierra Leone during the conflict. While Danny Archer returns from Cape Town after meeting Colonel Coetzee, the camera captures the scene from Freetown, the capital city as an unplanned city of a developing nation. Through the bird's eye shot, the film captures the rooftop setting of the city. Unmanaged bus stops, the old-turned vehicles, the frightened people, etc., are not beyond the reality of a war-torn country. In this sense, the contemporary social reality of Sierra Leone is the major concern of the cinema. The bird's eye shot is taken here to reflect the contemporary picture of Freetown.

Since the title of the cinema *Blood Diamond* refers to the diamond found by Solomon that has been hidden in the jungle, the film makes this stone central and makes other characters directly or indirectly connected with it. While Danny Archer knows the fact he is behind Solomon for the diamond. Similarly, the Colonel of RUF has kidnapped his son Dia and has made him a devoted rebel to bargain for a pink diamond with Solomon.

Because of the diamond, Solomon becomes one of the targeted persons for all others. Danny Archer not only meets Solomon but also tries to persuade him regarding diamonds. Just before the scene of the RUF attack on Freetown, Archer says to Solomon:

> Don't tell me you're gonna try to sell it yourself. To who? And for what price, my friend? You need my help, whether you like it or not. Here, let me help you with that. You hear that? You hear that? They come into the city overnight. It's started. What are you gonna do now, huh? Listen, the right stone can bring anything. Information. Safety. Even Freedom. (*Blood Diamond*)

In this sense, Danny Archer tries to convince Solomon of the diamond. Furthermore, he tells Solomon that even his existence is connected to that secret diamond. Danny Archer says, "But a big stone does not stay secret for very long." The moment you tell anyone about it, your life is worthless. The only reason you're alive is you haven't told anyone where it is" (*Blood Diamond*).

Death and Displacement of Commoners

Diamonds-small pieces of carbon with no great intrinsic value - have been the cause of widespread death, destruction, and misery for almost a decade in the small West African country of Sierra Leone. Through the 1990s, Sierra Leone's rebel war became a tragedy of major humanitarian, political, and historic proportions. A weak post-independence democracy was subverted in the 1960s and 1970s by corruption and despotism. Economic decline and military rule followed. The rebellion that began in 1991 was characterized by banditry and horrific brutality, wreaked primarily on civilians. Regarding the death of Sierra Leone's civil war lan Smillie Lansana Gberie and Ralph Hazleton write, "Between 1991 and 1999, the war claimed over 75,000 lives, caused half a million Sierra Leoneans to become refugees, and displaced half of the country's 4.5 million people" (2).

There is a war-torn situation in Sierra Leone in one scene of the film in one hand. On the other hand, the story of the diamond goes parallel through Solomon and his other family members. The lens of the camera captures his son who was a genius in studies is now forcefully kidnapped and recruited as a RUF soldier. On the other side, Solomon's wife and two other children are in the refugee camp. Since Solomon is unaware of the whereabouts of his all family members, for him the price of the stone becomes his approach to his family members. Once again the cinema captures the scene of the RUF attack at

Freetown. Before visualizing the attacking scene, the film goes through B. B. C. news:

> In Sierra Leone, R. U. F. forces have been sighted within ten kilometers of the capital city of Freetown. The minister of the interior has expressed confidence that the government troops can repel the attack. All foreign nationals are being advised to leave the country. There are also unconfirmed reports that attacks are being committed by both sides in the rapidly worsening situations. The UN has described the refugee situation as critical. (*Blood Diamond*)

With the new broadcast, the film captures the scene of the RUF attack on Freetown. The terrific attack kills hundreds of people.

Solomon and Archer hardly save their lives while RUF attacks Freetown. Solomon pathetically searches for the names of his family members on the refugee list but cannot find them. On the other side, Danny Archer takes an oath to help him to find his family.

Danny Archer meets a lady journalist girl named Maddy Bowen. Through Maddy Bowen, *Blood Diamond* implies a young, attractive female reporter who is not only afraid to use her sex appeal with Danny Archer but also able to take any risk for her profession of reporting in a critical war-torn country, Sierra Leone. She works for Time magazine as a foreign correspondent in *Blood Diamond*. In her pursuit of a story about conflict diamonds in Sierra Leone, she recognizes smuggler Danny Archer at a bar and proceeds to flirt with him.

Maddy Bowen does not identify herself as a reporter until Danny realizes she is a journalist when she asks him about *Blood Diamonds* but as a journalist, her help for both Solomon and Archer could not be marred. She not only helps Solomon to find his family but even to settle in London. Similarly, Archer too somehow succeeds his in mission due to the help of Maddy Bowen. She uses her resources as a reporter and helps Danny's friend Solomon find his son, who has been forced into the military as a child soldier. On the other hand, she even tries to find his other family members in the refugee camp of Tassin where Solomon's wife and two other children have been living while Solomon is hopelessly searching for missing family members.

Just after Solomon and Archer escape from Freetown after the terrifying attack by RUF, both of them meet Maddy Bowen. She leads them to the Tassin Refugee Camp, Forecariah, Guinea. The film captures the plights and suffering of thousands of displaced people of Sierra Leone in refugee camps with the story connected with Solomon's family. Subsequently, the cinema captures the mass of millions of people. Maddy Bowen remarks regarding the people of Tassin Refugee camp, "This is what a million people look like. At the moment, the second largest refugee camp of Africa" (*Blood Diamond*).

Maddy is critical of her line of work in the film as a journalist. For example, when Danny mocks Maddy for writing: about the image she took of Solomon reuniting with his wife and children at the Tassin Refugee Camp in Guinea, she replies at length:

REFLECTION OF HISTORY IN BLOOD DIAMOND: THE POWER OF CINEMA

Do you think I'm exploiting his grief? You're right. It's shit. It's like one of those infomercials. You know...with the little black babies with swollen bellies and flies in their eyes. And so here I've got dead mothers. I've got severed limbs. But it's nothing new. And it might be enough to make some people cry if they read, maybe even write a check. But it's not going to be enough to make it stop. I am sick of writing about victims, but it's all I can fucking do because I need facts. I need names. I need dates. I need pictures. I need bank accounts. People back home wouldn't buy a ring if they knew it cost someone else their hand. But I can't write that story until I get facts that can be verified, which is to say until I find someone who will go on record. (*Blood Diamond*)

Maddy seems much more professional in her work. Within the professionalism of journalism, the film reveals the bitter reality of the pain and suffering of the war victims and that their plights and suffering have become a profession for people like journalists. Due to such a chaotic situation, it becomes news, subject matter for writings issue of discussion, etc. Maddy is critical of her audience, and also her profession. Her speech vocalizes some of the setbacks she experiences as a photojournalist, claiming that she needs to provide her audience with more information to move them to action. Anyway, the film's effort to visualize the scene of the refugee camp can stand as the living history of Sierra Leone. The actual data of refugees of Sierra Leone is somehow captured in the film as Hoffman writes, "The civil war in Sierra Leone inflicted tremendous human suffering on the population. The death toll in the war is probably close to 75,000. Two million persons have been displaced and 20,000 mutilated" (212).

The war increased morbidity and mortality rates, particularly amongst the most vulnerable rural poor. It is, however, difficult to identify particular victims of this war. No specific ethnic group was targeted, and no horizontal inequalities were exploited to fuel the war. In this connection, Danny Hoffman writes, "The war has caused a tremendous refugee crisis and internal displacement. The below table represents the people fleeing the country, mostly to neighboring Guinea. It does not reflect the internally displaced persons. It is estimated that more than two-thirds of the population was displaced internally" (10). Since the setting of Tassin Refugee Camp of Guinea is realistically presented in the film, it captures the realistic social picture of historical facts in visual form.

An Attempt to Resolve the Conflict in Sierra Leone

Finally, the film gives justice to Solomon as he gets a diamond and reunites with his family members in London. But in doing so, he had gone through a very harsh life and struggle, Finally, both Danny Archer and Maddy Bowen help him to find his goal. Solomon while he meets his wife Jessie in the refugee camp knows his son has already been kidnapped by RUF. He cries loudly, "Where is my son? Oh Christ! Where is my son?" (*Blood Diamond*). Through Solomon and Jessie's cries, the film realistically captures the suffering of war victims.

Now only mission left for Solomon is to find out his son and for Archer the pink diamond. For the union of the family, Solomon is ready to sacrifice a diamond. On the other hand, both the RUF and Colonel have led their military troops to the diamond field where Solomon has hidden his diamond. Solomon disguises himself as the RUF soldier, enters to RUF camp, and finds his son playing cards with similar child soldiers. The hopeless situation occurs for Solomon when his son says to him, "Who are you? I don't know. You the fisherman" (*Blood Diamond*). Subsequently, his son appeals to his other child soldiers to kill him as an enemy of them. The true result of the manipulation and brainwashing of child soldiers is reflected in Solomon's son Dia's psychology. Luckily, due to a person who knows valuable diamonds, the commander of RUF does not let him kill.

On the other hand, Colonel Coetzee forces both Archer and Solomon for diamonds. While Solomon according to Archer's advice and plan pretends that the diamond has already been taken by others, at the moment he is nearly killed by Colonel Coetzee. While he quickly starts to dig out the diamond, Archer kills Colonel Coetzee but at that very moment, he is badly wounded by Colonel's bullet. Solomon's son Dia appears pistol-pointing it to Solomon and Archer. Luckily, Dia is convinced while both father's and son's eyes are filled with tears. Solomon gives a diamond to Archer and all three move from there. Archer due to his wound could not lead himself ahead and finally, he realizes his forthcoming death. He gives the diamond to Solomon and blocks another military of the Colonel's forces so that Solomon and Dia can go ahead safely. Archer at the eleventh hour of his death, calls Maddy Bowen and sends Solomon and Dia to London with the diamond.

The film brings the reality of Sierra Leone during the civil war parallel with the story of a large pink-colored diamond. The phrase "*Blood Diamond*" stands parallel with Sierra Leone's part of the history of the conflict as Iryna Marchuk writes:

> Despite its abundant natural resources, Sierra Leone experienced economic decline throughout the 1980s, due in large part to rampant corruption. Rich diamond mining areas fueled the conflict between various groups and individuals. The exploitation of diamond resources escalated to such an extent that the diamonds became known as 'blood diamonds." (87)

Keeping the remark of Iryna Marchuk into consideration, the title of the cinema *Blood Diamond* is not beyond the reality of Sierra Leone's history. Due to the effort of the film to bring the social, political, economic, and cultural reality of Sierra Leone, *Blood Diamond* stands as a living history of Sierra Leone's civil war. The film is a very successful attempt to change the image of diamonds by linking them explicitly to blood and depriving them of the same stroke of their innocence. A characteristic assessment of the film is that it succeeds in the actual visual representation of Sierra Leone's part of history.

The film, in the end, discloses the main cause of the illegal trade of diamonds while Maddy Bowen brings the reality to the media as she has the mission to capture the real process and root of illegal diamond supply from Sierra Leone to the Western world or final destination of diamonds. Maddy Bowen while knowing that Solomon has a pink diamond and searching for his family, not only brings him to London but also compels greedy businessman, Mr. Van De Kaap to bring and unite Solomon's family to get his diamond. Furthermore, Maddy Bowen, with the help of Solomon, captures the incident of how a big businessman like Mr. Van De Kaap buys such illegal diamonds from Sierra Leone. Finally, Van De Kaap is captured and disclosed for the illegal trade of diamonds but Solomon can establish his prosperous life. In this sense, the mission of Maddy Bowen to find the actual cause of the illegal diamond supply in Sierra Leone is presented by the cinema. The cinema conveys the message that to stop the violence in Sierra Leone there must be an abolishment of the illegal supply of diamonds which is one of the major historical realities faced by Sierra Leone during the last decade of the 20th century,

The final scene of the cinema portrays the role of journalists in dealing with the critical circumstances of war-torn scenarios. The photographs taken by Maddy Bowen help to unite Solomon's family as well as to catch the main destination of illegal diamonds. The film, as the major element, brings the attachment of Maddy Bowen and Danny Archer. The attachment of Maddy Bowen towards Danny Archer further inspires her to help Solomon and for her, Solomon could be a proper person to find the track of diamonds from Sierra Leone to the Western world.

Maddy Bowen, Danny Archer, and Solomon Vandy, all three are united due to the diamond. However, all have different purposes; Maddy Bowen aims to trace the reality of illegal diamond supply as a journalist, Danny Archer aims to get a diamond and secure his life, and Solomon with the help of diamonds aims to reunite all his family members. The triangular relation further helps to develop love between Bowen and Archer. The film gives justice to Solomon by reuniting his family and leading him to a prosperous life. It fulfills the mission of Maddy Bowen but Danny Archer faces a tragic death however his death seems heroic because due to Archer's help both Solomon and Bowen find their aims.

The love between Danny Archer and Maddy Bowen does not go long lasting since the protagonist dies but the film finds a happy ending for Solomon's family. As commercial cinema, the film goes through fairy tale elements such as the happy ending of the innocent, laborious, and hard-working common family of Solomon, the good result of risky journalism, and the tragic end of a greedy smuggler Danny Archer; all the cinematic events, incidents, and plots are not beyond the socio-political reality of Sierra Leone. The realistic representation of the film is nothing else but a representation of historical facts of the certain timeframe of the history of Sierra Leone in fictional form.

Chapter IV

Conclusion: A Call for Critical Assessment of History

Historical meta-fiction refers to a work of art especially literary or visual work which captures the historical sense of certain places and timeframes with the stress of realistic events and incidents. *Blood Diamond* is set in Sierra Leone during the civil war in 1999 and is not beyond the true historical facts of the nation. As its title indicates, it is a very explicit attempt to link blood and diamonds. The film connects both blood and diamonds with the history of Sierra Leone. Sierra Leone is well known for its diamond minerals. Much more than this, it is known for the continuous terror, violence, and tussle between rebels and the unstable government of the nation during the last decade of the 20th century. The film tries to address the conflict due to the valuable minerals like diamonds in the country.

With the continuous armed conflict, there is the death of thousands of innocent people, displacement of citizens as well as extreme suffering. These are the historical facts associated with Sierra Leone. *Blood Diamond* as a war and political adventure movie tries to visualize similar realistic incidents which have made it a reflection of Sierra Leone's part of history. *Blood Diamond* does so by systematically linking diamonds to blood and more generally to violence and war. The film presents diamonds as the driving factor of war. The trade of rough diamonds, as the film suggests, allows the RUF to finance the war. It is presented as the key motivation for rebellion in Sierra Leone. Through the visual language, the film also ties diamonds to particular exercises of physical violence in the war.

Diamonds are directly associated with the terror in the film. Similarly, the use of child soldiers, the enslavement of men for work in the diamond mines, and the massive displacement of the civilian population, etc., are not beyond the social and political reality of Sierra Leone. Not surprisingly, the first diamonds shown in the film are blood-stained. They are briefly shown when Archer gets them from RUF Commander Zero, in the close-up shot when one of the border guards shows them. These diamonds are sullied with blood, as the guard has just cut them out of the goat that Archer has used to smuggle them into Liberia. Symbolically the violence associated with diamonds is a historical fact of Sierra Leone.

To ensure that the message does not remain fiction, *Blood Diamond* operates a constant back-and-forth between objective facts and the fictional story. Sometimes the actors give factual accounts linking blood and diamonds. In her first encounter with Archer, for example, Bowen gives an overview of the diamond smuggling from Sierra Leone to Liberia. The film starts with black fact sheets locating Sierra Leone and tying diamonds with civil war. Similarly, a fictional rendering of a factual presentation at the 2000 G8 Ministerial Summit on trade in rough diamonds is inserted or juxtaposed to the attack on the Mende Village disrupting the family of Solomon.

Finally, the film discloses the main cause of the illegal trade of diamonds. Maddy Bowen brings the reality to media as she has the mission to capture the real process and root of illegal diamond supply from Sierra Leone. Maddy Bowen knows that Solomon has a pink diamond and searching for his family. She not only brings him to London but also compels greedy businessman, Mr. Van De Kaap to bring and unite Solomon's family. Maddy Bowen, with the help of Solomon, captures the incident of how a big businessman like Mr. Van De Kaap buys such illegal diamonds from Sierra Leone. It reveals Van De Kaap's real identity in the media as the diamond smuggler who has been playing a major role in the civil war in Sierra Leone.

As a commercial cinema, the film, as the major element, brings the attachment of Maddy Bowen and Danny Archer, the major factor in bringing them together is nothing else but diamonds. Maddy Bowen, Danny Archer, and Solomon Vandy, all three are united due to the diamond with different purposes. Maddy Bowen aims to reveal the reality of illegal diamond supply. Similarly, Danny Archer aims to get a diamond and to make his life secure. Solomon with the help of a diamond wants to reunite all his family members. The film gives justice to Solomon by reuniting his family. It even fulfills the mission of Maddy Bowen but Danny Archer faces a tragic death however his death seems heroic.

The film finds a happy ending for Solomon's family and Maddy Bowen too accomplishes her mission with the help of Danny Archer however, it ends with the tragic death of Danny Archer and the tragic end of their love story. Through the triangular relationship among a diamond smuggler, Danny Archer, journalist, Maddy Bowen, and common native Solomon Vandy, the film establishes itself as a commercial success cinema for common audiences but also stands as a historical meta-fiction due to its representation of historical facts of the last decade of 20th century from Sierra Leone's history in fictional form. The message of the film seems to its audience that they have just seen a good action movie with a romantic plot, but the film also makes the audience think differently about diamonds and wars with historical knowledge of Sierra Leone's civil war. The filmmakers have conquered the place and time frame of Sierra Leone's part of history as a cluttered landscape like historians, anthropologists, and sociologists. In this sense, *Blood Diamond* is a historical meta-fiction that depicts a certain part of Sierra Leone's history in fictional representation as a call for the critical assessment of history.

Works Cited

Abdullah, Ibrahim. "Bushpath to Destruction: The Origin and Character of the Revolutionary

United Front." *African Development* XXII. 3/4 (1997): 45-76.

Abrams, M. H. 4 *Glossary of Literary Terms*. Bangalore: Harcourt, 2005.

Adams, Hazard, ed. *Critical Theory Since Plato*. Rev. ed. New York: Harcourt, 1992.

Barker, Chris. *The Sage Dictionary of Cultural Studies*, London: Sage Publication, 2004.

Barry, Peter. *Beginning Theory: An Introduction to Literacy and Cultural Theory*. Manchester:

Manchester UP, 1995.

Coulter, Chris, "The Post-War Moment: Female Fighters in Sierra Leone." *Migration Studies*.

Working Paper Series 22. Forced Migration Studies Programme, University of the

Witwatersrand, 2005. Web. 20 Nov. 2014.

<http://migration.wits.ac.za/CoulterWP.pdf>.

Foucault, Michel. "Nietzsche, Genealogy and History." *The Foucault Reader.* Trans. Poul

Rabinow. New York: Pantheon, 1984. 76-100.

—-. "Truth and Power." Adams 1135-45.

Ginifer, Jeremy, and Kaye Oliver. *Evaluation of the Conflict Prevention Pools*:

Country/Regional Case Study Sierra Leone. Department for International Development,

United Kingdom, 2004. Web. 23 Nov. 2014.

<http://www.dfid.gov.uk/aboutdfid/performance/files/ ev647sleone.pdf>.

Greenblatt, Stephen. "The Improvisation of Power." *Renaissance Self-Fashioning.*

. London: National Gallery, 1980. 1-18.

—-. *Renaissance Self-Fashioning.* London: National Gallery, 1980,

Hoffman, Danny. "The Civilian Target in Sierra Leone and Liberia: Political Power, Military

Strategy, and Humanitarian Intervention." *African Affairs.* 103,4 (2004): 211-226.

Marchuk, Iryna. "Confronting *Blood Diamond*s in Sierra Leone: The Trial of Charles Taylor."

Yale Journal of International Affairs 4. 2 (Spring-Summer, 2009): 87-99.

Milan, Alexa. "Modern Portrayals of Journalism in Film." *The Eton Journal of Undergraduate*

Research in Communications 1.1 (Winter 2010): 46-57.

Montrose, Louis. "New Historicism." *Redrawing the Boundaries.* Ed. Stephen Greenblatt and

Giles Gunn. New York: MLA 1992, 392-418.

Mwakawago, Daudi. *As Peacekeepers Depart Sierra Leone: Numerous Challenges Remain.* UN

official: UN News Centre. 3 Oct. 2005. Web. 25 Nov. 2014. <www.un.org/apps/news/ story.asp?NewsID-16077&Cr-sierra&Crl-leone[1]>.

Nietzsche, Frederick. "Truth and Falsity in Ultramoral Sense." Adams 634-39.

---

[1]	http://www.un.org/apps/news/story.asp?NewsID-16077&Cr-sierra&Crl-leone

Orgel, Stephen. "The Role of King." Ed. H. Aram Veeser. *The New Historicism Reader*. London:
Routledge, 1994. 370-75,
Peters, Krijn. *Re-Examining Voluntarism: Youth Combatants in Sierra Leone*. Pretoria: Institute
for Security Studies, 2004.
Puig, Claudia "*Blood Diamond* Shines Forth." USA Today 7 Dec. 2006: 8-9.
Rainer, Peter. "Star-studded, Flawed Diamond." *Christian Science Monitor*. 8 Dec 2006. Web.
24 Sept. 2014.
<http://www.csmonitor.com/World/Making-a-difference/2014/1229/>
Rebecca, Winters Keegan. "Can A Film Change The World?" *Time* 14.3 (March 2008): 60-61.
Richards, Paul. "To Fight or to Farm? Agrarian Dimensions of the Mano River Conflicts (Liberia
and Sierra Leone)." *African Affairs* 104.3 (2005): 571-90.
Rodney, Walter. *How Europe Underdeveloped Africa*. Guyana: City Press, 1985.
Said, Edward W. *Orientalism*, New York: Alfred A. Knopf, 1993.
Slemen, Stephen. *A Postmodern Reader*. New York: State University Press, 1993.
Smillie, Ian, Lansana Gberie, and Ralph Hazleton. *The Heart of the Matter Sierra Leone.*
Diamonds & Human Security (Complete Report). Ottawa: Partnership Africa Canada,
2000.

Steams, Peter N., Peters Seixas, and Sam Wineburg. *Knowing Teaching and Learning History:*

National and International Perspectives. New York: New York University Press, 2000,

Tyson, Lois. "New Historicism and Cultural Materialism." *Critical Theory Today.* Ed. Lois

Tyson. New York, London: Garland Publishing, 1999: 277-316.

Veenstra, Jan R. "The New Historicism of Stephen Greenblatt: On Poetics of Culture and the

Interpretation of Shakespeare." *History and Theory* 34.3 (Oct 1995): Ed. Jan R. Veenstra

and Others, 174-98.

Veeser, H. Aram. *The New Historicism Reader.* New York: Routledge, 1994.

Voeltz, Richard. "Africa, Buddies, Diamonds, Politics, and Gold: A Comparison of the Films

Blood Diamond (2006) and Gold! (1974)." *Nebula* 7.1/7.2 (June 2010): 186-97.

Zwick, Edward, et al., Dr. *Blood Diamond.* Burbank, CA: Warner Bros. Pictures, 2007.

ABOUT THE AUTHOR

DB Thakuri, born in Palpa, Nepal, is a highly accomplished author, screenwriter, script consultant, and film director with over a decade of experience in filmmaking. He holds a Master of Arts degree from Tribhuvan University. As a member of the Film Directors' Guild of Nepal since 2010, Thakuri has been an integral part of the filmmaking community. Thakuri imparts his expertise to aspiring filmmakers through guest lectures at various academic institutions. Additionally, he has authored the book *"Headwaters of Screenwriting: The Art of Crafting Original Screenplays."* which explores eternal principles and theory of crafting a truly compelling and original screenplay.

Beyond his professional endeavors, Thakuri loves football, mountains, and eternal solitude.

Email: infodbthakuri@gmail.com

www.dbthakuri.com[2]

---

2.   http://www.dbthakuri.com/

Don't miss out!

Visit the website below and you can sign up to receive emails whenever DB Thakuri publishes a new book. There's no charge and no obligation.

https://books2read.com/r/B-A-SAZAB-EIIPC

Connecting independent readers to independent writers.

Also by DB Thakuri

Reflection of History in Blood Diamond: The Power of Cinema

Reflection of History in Blood Diamond: The Power of Cinema

Headwaters of Screenwriting: The Art of Crafting Original Screenplays

About the Author

DB Thakuri, born in Palpa, Nepal, is a highly accomplished author, screenwriter, script consultant, and film director with over a decade of experience in filmmaking. He holds a Master of Arts degree from Tribhuvan University. As a member of the Film Directors' Guild of Nepal since 2010, Thakuri has been an integral part of the filmmaking community. Thakuri imparts his expertise to aspiring filmmakers through guest lectures at various academic institutions. Additionally, he has authored the book "Headwaters of Screenwriting: The Art of Crafting Original Screenplays" and " Reflection of History in Blood Diamond: The Power of Cinema."

Beyond his professional endeavors, Thakuri loves football, mountains, and eternal solitude.

Email: infodbthakuri@gmail.comw

ww.dbthakuri.com

Read more at www.dbthakuri.com.

www.ingramcontent.com/pod-product-compliance
Lightning Source LLC
Chambersburg PA
CBHW031444130726
47989CB00003B/1279